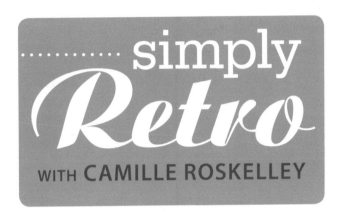

simply
Retro
WITH **CAMILLE ROSKELLEY**

· Fresh Quilts from Classic Blocks ·

Use Precut
Jelly Rolls,
Charm Packs,
Fat Quarters
& More

stashBOOKS.

an imprint of C&T Publishing

PUBLISHER: Amy Marson

CREATIVE DIRECTOR: Gailen Runge

ART DIRECTOR / BOOK DESIGNER: Kristy Zacharias

EDITOR: Cynthia Bix

TECHNICAL EDITORS: Teresa Stroin and Doreen Hazel

PRODUCTION COORDINATOR: Zinnia Heinzmann

PRODUCTION EDITOR: Alice Mace Nakanishi

ILLUSTRATOR: Jessica Jenkins

PHOTO ASSISTANT: Mary Peyton Peppo

FLAT QUILT PHOTOGRAPHY by Christina Carty-Francis and Diane Pedersen of C&T Publishing, Inc., unless otherwise noted

STYLE PHOTOGRAPHY by Camille Roskelley, unless otherwise noted

Published by Stash Books, an imprint of C&T Publishing, Inc., P.O. Box 1456, Lafayette, CA 94549

Library of Congress Cataloging-in-Publication Data

Roskelley, Camille.

  Simply retro with Camille Roskelley : fresh quilts from classic blocks / Camille Roskelley.

    pages cm

  ISBN 978-1-60705-684-3 (soft cover)

1. Patchwork--Patterns. 2. Quilting--Patterns. I. Title.

TT835.R6746 2013

746.46--dc23

                    2012042245

Printed in China

10 9 8 7 6 5 4 3 2 1

DEDICATION

For my boys. All four of them. The biggest one for the love, support, encouragement, and takeout. The next one for being such a great helper with his little brothers. The little one for complimenting every single thing that comes from my sewing room and giving me more hugs than any mom could ask for. And the littlest one for playing with Charm Packs and Jelly Rolls like blocks and for snuggling with me when I am too tired to sew another stitch.

For my parents, who taught me how to work my guts out and love what I do. For my family, who made me who I am. For my friends near and far, those I've met and those I haven't, who cheer me on day after day.

Love to you all.

I'm the luckiest girl in the world.

ACKNOWLEDGMENTS

An enormous thank-you to:

My Moda family, for the opportunities that you have given me and the chance to do something I absolutely love. For the boxes and boxes of the most beautiful fabric and then some. Lissa, Cheryl, Mark, all the reps, and the designers and crew, thank you. Really.

The lovely staff at C&T Publishing, who worked as hard as I did making this book a reality. Susanne, Cynthia, Teresa, Kristy, and every person there who so graciously put up with my many ideas and even more opinions. You've been amazing.

My sewing night girls. You keep me going and remind me how much I love what I do. Not to mention the treats.

And my mom, who taught me everything I know and always, always answers the phone when I need help with the slow cooker.

contents

introduction

The concept of "retro" is pretty wonderful; it means "reminiscent of things past." Isn't that appropriate for quilting?

I come from a long line of quilters. In fact, my quilting roots go all the way back to my pioneer ancestors who stitched by the fire at night, their hands never idle, making beautiful, sometimes unbelievably intricate quilts to keep their loved ones warm at night. From those pioneer women, and from grandmas and mothers, comes something rooted in a love of all things quilting and creative.

Those early quilters didn't have rotary blades, cutting mats, or even sewing machines, but they certainly had wonderful imaginations. Thousands upon thousands of beautiful quilt blocks can be traced back to these women, and many—if not most—of our favorite blocks today can be attributed to them.

Things have changed a lot over the years. We have so many wonderful tools to make our quilting lives easier, and we have beautiful, time-saving, precut fabrics to work with! We've also come up with lots of new ways of doing things while still remembering our roots.

The blocks for the quilts in this book are a delightful mix of classic blocks, updated blocks, and blocks that combine traditional elements to create a fresh, yet retro look. For example, I absolutely love to make baby quilts using just one traditional quilt block, but using it nice and big! It makes the traditional block feel new and fresh and is a great way to showcase the newest fabrics.

You can see this at work in the *Baby Love* quilts that are based on the Churn Dash block. In one version is a traditional 12˝ block that is repeated, but in the other version is a jumbo-size block that feels much more modern.

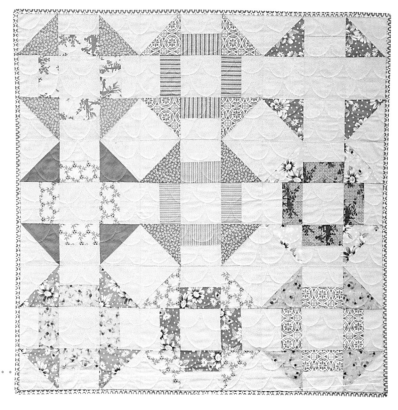

Baby Love *made with 12˝ blocks (project on page 29)*

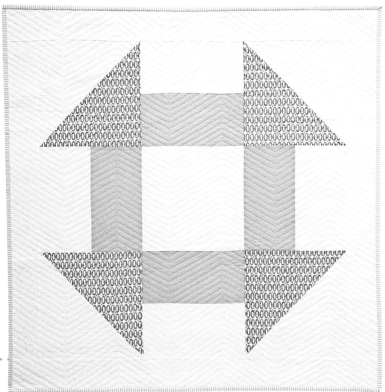

Baby Love *made with one 30˝ block (project on page 33)*

Another change from those early quilting days is the ways in which we've learned how to simplify: Instead of Y-seams and foundation piecing, I'll show you how to use simple half-square triangles (HSTs), Flying Geese units, and chain piecing (I'm a big fan of chain piecing!) to make blocks that only look complicated. The piecing, combined with clever placement of light and dark fabrics, creates interesting secondary designs in many of these quilts. Those concepts, combined with fresh, modern fabric, are part of what makes a traditional block that feels "new" again.

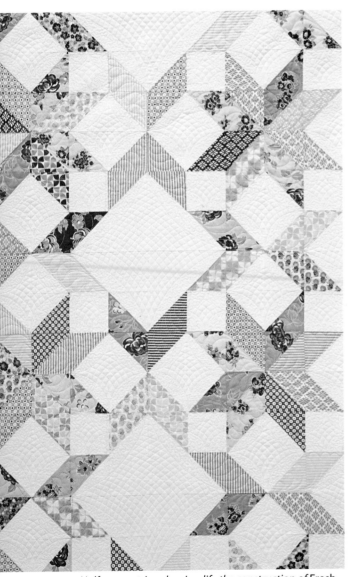

Half-square triangles simplify the construction of Fresh *(full quilt on page 89).*

Flying Geese were used in Sweet Life *(full quilt on page 75).*

Swoon, 2011, designed by Camille Roskelley

Note: Swoon is available as both a paper and PDF pattern in my shop at thimbleblossoms.com and in local quilt shops everywhere.

One of my very favorite quilts, *Swoon*, was inspired by a beautiful antique quilt I stumbled upon one day. The original quilt was gorgeous, but making it as it was originally constructed required difficult-to-piece Y-seams and templates. I spent the next few days reworking the block to make it simple-to-piece, fat-quarter friendly, and *big*. I loved the way the large scale and color placement made an otherwise traditional block look bold and updated. I swooned. And so did many of you!

A Flickr group, perfectly named The *Swoon*-along, was started by Katy Jones. The group filled with thousands of *Swoon* blocks. *Swoon* quilts started popping up, made from every fabric and every color palette imaginable.

And that is how this book was born— traditional blocks, with a bold twist, updated, some of them large, some enormous. All favorites. And you can make them too.

While this book includes my interpretation of many of these traditional blocks, it certainly wouldn't have been possible without those women of days past, who wanted to make their homes and the lives of their families more beautiful, just as we do today. To them I express my utmost gratitude. For seeing the possibilities in sewing together tiny pieces of fabric, for creating such a beautiful way to express themselves, and especially for teaching their daughters.

A Word about *Fabric*

Seasoned quilters and beginners alike can sometimes find it challenging to select fabrics for a quilt from the huge array offered at the local quilt store. When I first began quilting, fabric selection seemed a little overwhelming. Then somewhere along the line I was introduced to a Charm Pack. I fell in love immediately! Each and every square in the little pack complemented the others beautifully. Genius. On occasion, I still enjoy selecting fabric based on pattern, scale, and color. But for my design style, I usually stick with using one main fabric collection with a few unexpected pieces mixed in.

CUT GOODS RUNDOWN

Whether or not you like making your own fabric selections, it's tough to beat the convenience of cut goods (also called precuts). The term "cut goods" generally refers to a specific fabric collection, or line, that is cut to a specific dimension. For example, the Ruby fabric line—which my mother, Bonnie Olaveson, and I designed for Moda—had 40 coordinating prints. A Ruby Charm Pack included 42 precut squares 5″ × 5″, all ready to be sewn.

The quilts in this book are made with both yardage and cut goods, or precuts. Here, I'll give you a rundown of the kinds of precuts you can use in these projects.

fyi

There's no need to prewash your cut goods. Just start sewing! Simple as that.

Fat Quarter Bundles

Charm Packs

Charm Packs

These are 5″ × 5″ squares of coordinating fabric from the same fabric collection. Charm Packs include one of each of the prints, usually 25–42 squares. The number of squares in a pack is typically stated on the back.

Layer Cakes

With these, it's a snap to throw together a quick and easy quilt. Layer Cakes are 10″ × 10″ squares from one fabric collection. They include 42 squares.

Layer Cakes

Jelly Rolls

I love Jelly Rolls! You can combine them in so many ways to make a huge variety of blocks. A Jelly Roll is 40 strips 2½″ × 45″ from one line of fabric. I just like seeing them stacked on my shelf, all rolled up and looking so darned cute!

Jelly Rolls

Fat Quarter Bundles

Generous pieces, but not too big. And *so* versatile. Fat quarter bundles include as many fat quarters as there are prints in one collection. What is a fat quarter? Well, if you cut ¼ yard of fabric, it would measure 9″ × 44″. So you'd have a long skinny quarter-yard. Instead, a fat quarter is 18″ × 22″. Half the width, twice the length—still a quarter-yard.

A FEW BASICS

Every quilt in this book was made from premium-quality 100% cotton. Although many of the fabrics shown are unavailable now (fabric manufacturers keep most fabrics in print for only a short time), you can most likely find similar fabrics at your local quilt store.

For the white neutral solid fabric in the projects, I used a Moda Bella Solid in Bleached White. I love this white solid so much that I buy it by the bolt!

In the quilt projects, *WOF* means width of fabric. One yard of fabric is 36″ × 45″. Most fabric is considered to be 44″–45″ wide, but because it isn't usually quite that, I assume 42″ to be safe. So yardage amounts given in the quilt projects are based on 42″-wide fabric. If your fabric is 45″ wide, there is no need to trim it to 42″.

THREAD

For quilting, I use 100% cotton thread because I use 100% cotton fabric. I especially enjoy using Aurifil 100% cotton thread; I've had great luck with it.

The *Projects*

Swell

I have a pretty healthy fabric stash. I love it to pieces. It's a little embarrassing, really, how many times I've folded and organized all of it. There is just something about all those different fabrics playing so happily together. This quilt seems so cheery to me, with all its different fabrics and so many of my favorite prints. Besides, who wouldn't want to wrap up in cheeriness every day?

Pieced by Camille Roskelley and quilted by Angela Walters

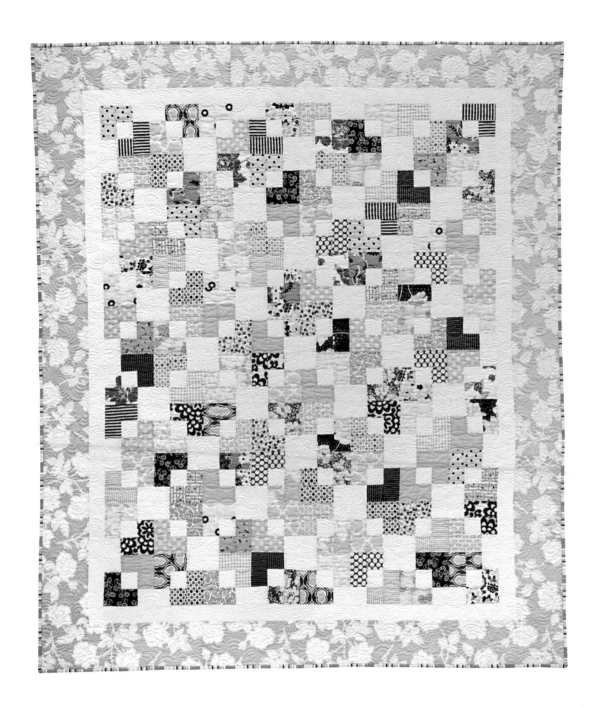

FINISHED QUILT: 63″ × 75″ | FINISHED BLOCK: 12″ × 12″

FABRIC: Prints from my stash

Materials

Yardages are based on 42"-wide fabric.

- 32 strips of print fabric 2½" × WOF* for the blocks**

- 1¾ yards of white fabric for the blocks and inner border

- 1¼ yards of print fabric for the outer border

- 4 yards of fabric for the backing

- ⅝ yard of fabric for the binding

- 67" × 79" piece of cotton batting

WOF = width of fabric
*** Cut from yardage or use part of a Jelly Roll.*

Cutting

From *each* print strip:
Subcut pieces 2½" × 4½" (5 per strip, for a total of 160) for the blocks.

Subcut squares 2½" × 2½" (5 per strip, for a total of 160) for the blocks.

From white fabric:
Cut 15 strips 2½" × WOF; subcut squares 2½" × 2½" (16 per strip, for a total of 240) for the blocks.

Cut 6 strips 2½" × WOF for the inner border.

From print border fabric:
Cut 7 strips 6" × WOF for the outer border.

From binding fabric:
Cut 7 strips 2½" × WOF.

clever cutting

Cutting 2½"-wide strips from a big stack of your favorite prints is a great way to use your stash and make a one-of-a-kind quilt. Best of all, it gives you an excellent reason to go get more fabric!

BLOCK ASSEMBLY

1. Each block is made up of 4 units. For each unit, select 1 piece 2½″ × 4½″ and 1 square 2½″ × 2½″ from a print. Select the same pairing of pieces for another print. Add 3 squares 2½″ × 2½″ of the white fabric.

2. Follow the unit assembly diagram to sew the pieces in rows. Press. Then sew the rows together to make 1 unit. Press. Make 4 units.

3. Sew together the units as shown in the block assembly diagram, and press. Make 20 blocks.

Unit assembly

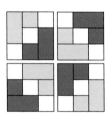

Block assembly

QUILT ASSEMBLY

1. Sew the blocks in 5 rows of 4 blocks each; press. Sew the rows together.

2. For the inner border, measure your quilt and follow the process in Tackling Borders (page 101), or use your favorite method for sewing squared borders.

3. Repeat Step 2 to add the outer border.

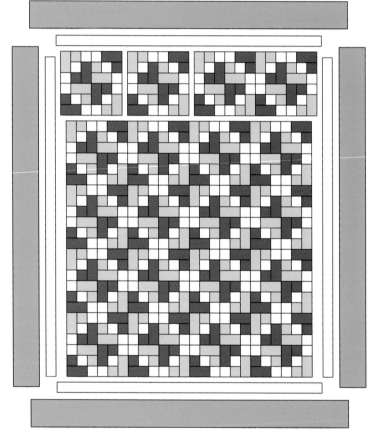

Quilt assembly

FINISHING

Use your favorite methods, or see Finish It! (page 101).

1. Cut the backing into 2 equal lengths (roughly 67″), and sew them together as described in Backing (page 103).

2. Layer the quilt top, batting, and backing, and pin baste to make a quilt sandwich. Machine or hand quilt as desired. Bind your quilt.

Retro

My great-grandma Ruby was quite a character. At a whopping 5'1" tall, she had bright red hair and drove a sporty orange Nova in her 70s. That sums her up pretty well. She was a fireball! We used one of her favorite aqua flower brooches, a vintage necklace I found at a flea market, and several classic prints from her fabric collection as the inspiration for the Ruby fabric line. It absolutely had to include red, aqua, and a bit of orange to commemorate the Nova. The same concepts apply to the quilt. Keep it simple and retro, aqua and white, with a little Ruby spunk thrown in. Just for fun.

Pieced and quilted by Camille Roskelley

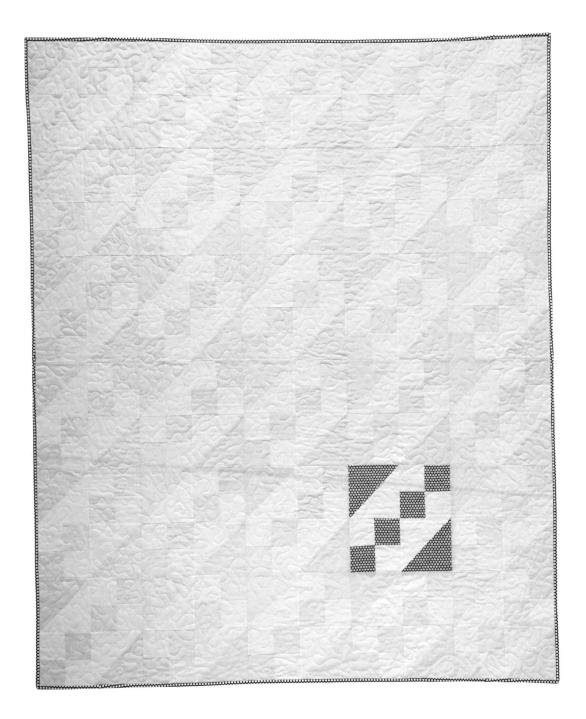

FINISHED QUILT: 60″ × 72″ | FINISHED BLOCK: 12″ × 12″

FABRIC: Ruby and Bliss by Bonnie and Camille for Moda

Materials

Yardages are based on 42″-wide fabric.

- 2½ yards of aqua fabric for the blocks

- 2½ yards of white fabric for the blocks

- 1 fat quarter of red fabric for the accent block*

- 3⅞ yards of fabric for the backing

- ⅝ yard of fabric for the binding

- 64″ × 76″ piece of cotton batting

* If you decide to skip the red block and make them all aqua, there is enough yardage to do so.

Cutting

From aqua fabric:

Cut 11 strips 3½″ × WOF;* subcut squares 3½″ × 3½″ (11 per strip, for a total of 116).

Cut 5 strips 6⅞″ × WOF; subcut squares 6⅞″ × 6⅞″ (6 per strip, for a total of 29).

From white fabric:

Cut 11 strips 3½″ × WOF; subcut squares 3½″ × 3½″ (11 per strip, for a total of 120).

Cut 5 strips 6⅞″ × WOF; subcut squares 6⅞″ × 6⅞″ (6 per strip, for a total of 30).

From red fabric:

Cut 4 squares 3½″ × 3½″.

Cut 1 square 6⅞″ × 6⅞″.

From binding fabric:

Cut 7 strips 2½″ × WOF.

* WOF = width of fabric

quick piecing

Chain piecing (page 100) makes quick work of this simple quilt. Make all the four-patches in one batch and all the half-square triangles in another. Snip them apart, press, and sew your blocks. You'll be a chain piecer in no time, and there's no going back!

BLOCK ASSEMBLY

Each block is made up of 2 four-patches and 2 half-square triangles (HSTs).

1. For each four-patch, select 2 aqua squares 3½″ × 3½″ and 2 white squares 3½″ × 3½″. Following the four-patch unit assembly diagram, sew together 2 aqua/white pairs, and press the seams toward the aqua. Sew the rows together; press. Make a total of 58 aqua four-patches and 2 red ones.

Four-patch assembly

2. To make the HSTs, refer to Easy HSTs (below). Pair aqua and white or red and white squares 6⅞″ × 6⅞″. Make a total of 58 aqua HSTs and 2 red ones.

3. Sew 1 HST to 1 four-patch to make 1 unit as shown in the block assembly diagram. Make 2; press. Sew the 2 units together to make 1 block. Make a total of 30 blocks—29 aqua and 1 red.

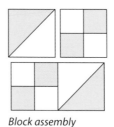

Block assembly

easy HSTs

Several quilts in this book feature blocks made with half-square triangles (HSTs). These are super easy to make. Here's the method.

An HST is made with 2 contrasting squares of the same size. Place 1 square on top of the other with right sides together (a). On the back of the lighter square, draw a pencil line from one corner to the opposite corner (b). Sew ¼″ from the line on each side (c). Cut on the line to make 2 HSTs (d). Press toward the darker of the 2 fabrics. Presto!

(a)

(b)

(c)

(d)

QUILT ASSEMBLY

1. Sew together the blocks in 6 rows of 5, with the red block in row 5, as shown in the quilt assembly diagram. Press.

2. Sew the rows together, and press.

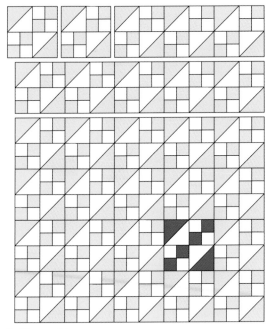

Quilt assembly

FINISHING

Use your favorite methods, or see Finish It! (page 101).

1. Cut the backing fabric into 2 equal lengths (roughly 64˝), and sew them together as described in Backing (page 103).

2. Layer the quilt top, batting, and backing, and pin baste to make a quilt sandwich. Machine or hand quilt as desired. Bind your quilt.

Baby Love

Baby quilts are one of my very favorite things to make. They are small, and they come together quickly. They also give me a chance to try lots of different designs and fabrics. For this project I made two different quilts, with two different takes on the same block. The small blocks quilt (page 29) is a nine-block version. The large block quilt (page 33) is a single big block.

Making one of your favorite blocks jumbo sized is a great option for a baby quilt. Size the block around 30″ × 30″, and add a 3″ border all the way around. These quilts feature a 12″ × 12″ block and an extra-large 30″ × 30″ block. I can't wait to see sweet little babies all wrapped up in them!

Pieced and quilted by Camille Roskelley

Small Blocks Quilt

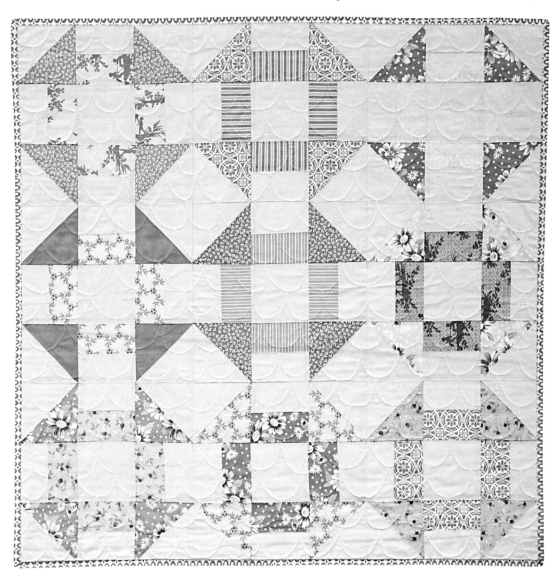

FINISHED QUILT: 36″ × 36″ | **FINISHED BLOCK:** 12″ × 12″

FABRIC: California Girl by Fig Tree & Co. for Moda

Materials

Yardages are based on 42″-wide fabric.

- 2 Charm Packs, or 18 pairs of matching 5″ × 5″ squares, for the blocks

- 1 yard of white fabric for the blocks

- 1¼ yards of fabric for the backing

- ⅓ yard of fabric for the binding

- 40″ × 40″ piece of cotton batting

Cutting

Select 18 pairs of matching Charm Squares. Cut each square into 2 pieces 2½″ × 4½″.

From white fabric:

Cut 3 strips 5″ × WOF;* subcut squares 5″ × 5″ (8 per strip, for a total of 18) for the blocks.

Cut 1 strip 4½″ × WOF; subcut squares 4½″ × 4½″ (a total of 9) for the blocks.

Cut 4 strips 2½″ × WOF; subcut pieces 2½″ × 4½″ (9 per strip, for a total of 36) for the blocks.

From binding fabric:

Cut 4 strips 2½″ × WOF.

* WOF = width of fabric

BLOCK ASSEMBLY

Each block is made up of 1 white square 4½″ × 4½″, 4 matching half-square triangles (HSTs), and 4 matching units 4½″ × 4½″.

1. Sew 1 Charm Square piece 2½″ × 4½″ to 1 white piece 2½″ × 4½″ to make 1 unit 4½″ × 4½″. Press. Repeat to make a total of 4 matching units.

2. Place 1 Charm Square 5″ × 5″ on top of 1 white square 5″ × 5″, right sides together. Make 2 HSTs. For directions, see Easy HSTs (page 26). Repeat with another set of squares to make a total of 4 matching HSTs. Press, and trim each to 4½″ × 4½″.

3. Sew 3 rows of 3 as shown in the block assembly diagram. Sew the rows together to make 1 block. Press.

4. Repeat Steps 1–3 to make a total of 9 blocks.

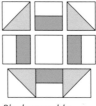

Block assembly

QUILT ASSEMBLY

Sew together the blocks in 3 rows of 3. Press. Sew together the rows as shown in the quilt assembly diagram.

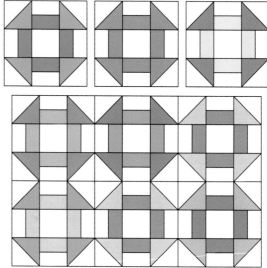

Quilt assembly

FINISHING

Use your favorite methods, or see Finish It! (page 101).

1. Make the backing as described in Backing (page 103).

2. Layer the quilt top, batting, and backing, and pin baste to make a quilt sandwich. Machine or hand quilt as desired. Bind your quilt.

Large Block Quilt

Pieced and quilted by Camille Roskelley

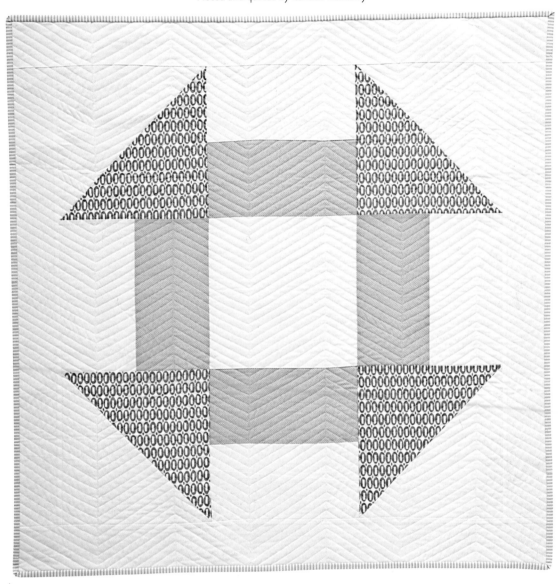

FINISHED QUILT: 36″ × 36″ | **FINISHED BLOCK:** 30″ × 30″

FABRIC: Pezzy Print by American Jane for Moda,
and Ruby by Bonnie and Camille for Moda

Materials

Yardages are based on 42″-wide fabric.

- ⅓ yard of solid fabric for the block

- ⅓ yard of coordinating print fabric for the block

- 1¼ yards of white fabric for the block and border

- 1¼ yards of fabric for the backing

- ⅓ yard of fabric for the binding

- 40″ × 40″ piece of cotton batting

Cutting

From solid fabric:
Cut 4 pieces 5½″ × 10½″.

From coordinating print fabric:
Cut 2 squares 10⅞″ × 10⅞″.

From white fabric:
Cut 2 squares 10⅞″ × 10⅞″.

Cut 4 pieces 5½″ × 10½″.

Cut 1 square 10½″ × 10½″.

Cut 4 strips 3½″ × WOF* for the border.

From binding fabric:
Cut 4 strips 2½″ × WOF.

* WOF = width of fabric

QUILT ASSEMBLY

This quilt top is a single large block. The block is just a jumbo version of the block used in the small blocks quilt (page 29). It is made up of 1 white square 10½″ × 10½″, 4 matching units 10½″ × 10½″, and 4 matching HSTs.

1. Sew 1 solid fabric piece 5½″ × 10½″ to 1 white piece 5½″ × 10½″ to make 1 unit 10½″ × 10½″. Press. Repeat to make a total of 4 matching units.

2. Place 1 coordinating print square 10⅞″ × 10⅞″ on top of 1 white square 10⅞″ × 10⅞″, right sides together. Make 2 HSTs. For directions, see Easy HSTs (page 26). Repeat with another set of squares to make a total of 4 matching HSTs. Press. At this point, the HSTs should measure 10½″ × 10½″.

3. Refer to the block assembly diagram for the small blocks quilt (page 30) to sew together 3 rows of 3. Press. Sew the rows together to make 1 large block. Press.

4. For the border, measure your quilt and follow the process in Tackling Borders (page 101), or use your favorite method for sewing squared borders.

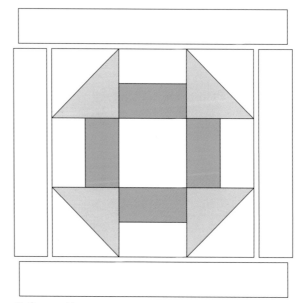

Quilt assembly

FINISHING

Use your favorite methods, or see Finish It! (page 101).

1. Make the backing as described in Backing (page 103).

2. Layer the quilt top, batting, and backing, and pin baste to make a quilt sandwich. Machine or hand quilt as desired. Bind your quilt.

quilting play

With small baby quilts, you can have fun experimenting with different quilting techniques. When I was quilting these, I used two quilting styles I hadn't ever tried. On the small blocks quilt, I stitched scallops. For the large block quilt, I did straight-line quilting in an allover zigzag pattern that added a modern touch. I loved the results!

Vintage

Someday when I learn to knit and crochet, I am going to make a granny square throw. But until that day, and as long as I have this brain and these fingers, I'm going to have to settle for some extra-large granny square quilt blocks. This block is such a delight to piece, and it's the perfect quilt for a twin-size bed. There is just something so fresh, yet so retro and classic, about the red and gray together on the white. A classic block in a few favorite colors. So simple, so clean, so retro.

Pieced by Camille Roskelley and quilted by Andrea Marquez

FINISHED QUILT: 65¼″ × 85″ | FINISHED BLOCK: 19¾″ × 19¾″

FABRIC: Ruby and Bliss by Bonnie and Camille for Moda

Materials

Yardages are based on 42″-wide fabric.

- 12 fat quarters or 12 quarter-yards of coordinating fabrics for the blocks

- 4 yards of white fabric for the blocks and border

- 5⅛ yards of fabric for the backing

- ⅝ yard of fabric for the binding

- 69″ × 89″ piece of cotton batting

Cutting

From *each* fat quarter or ¼-yard piece:*

Cut 2 squares 4″ × 4″.

Cut 2 strips 4″ × 11″.

Cut 6 pieces 4″ × 7½″.

From white fabric:

Cut 26 strips 4″ × WOF** for the blocks.

- From 4 strips, subcut pieces 4″ × 11″ (3 per strip, for a total of 12).

- From 22 strips, subcut squares 4″ × 4″ (10 per strip, for a total of 216).

Cut 8 strips 3½″ × WOF for the borders.

From binding fabric:

Cut 8 strips 2½″ × WOF.

* Refer to the cutting diagrams for help.
** WOF = width of fabric

Fat quarter cutting

Quarter-yard cutting

BLOCK ASSEMBLY

1. For each block, select the 10 pieces all cut from 1 fat quarter, 18 white squares 4″ × 4″, and 1 white rectangle 4″ × 11″. Refer to the block assembly diagram to arrange and sew together the block rows. Press.

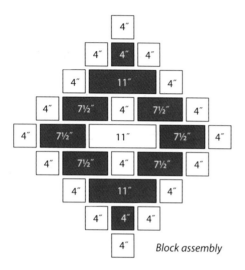

Block assembly

2. Sew the rows together to make 1 block.

a little tip

When you are sewing rows together, each white square should overlap the white square below it by ¼″.

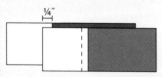

3. Press the block seams in the direction shown on the diagram.

4. Repeat Steps 1–3 to make a total of 12 blocks.

5. Trim each block to 20¼″ × 20¼″. Be careful to leave ¼″ beyond the points. You don't want to lose those pretty points in your seam allowance!

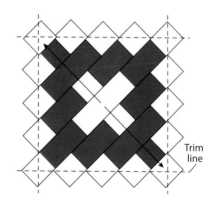

Trim line

QUILT ASSEMBLY

1. Sew the blocks into 4 rows of 3 blocks each. Press. Sew the rows together, and press.

2. For the border, measure the quilt and follow the process in Tackling Borders (page 101), or use your favorite method for sewing squared borders.

Quilt assembly

FINISHING

Use your favorite methods, or see Finish It! (page 101).

1. Cut the backing fabric into 2 equal lengths (roughly 89″), and sew them together as described in Backing (page 103).

2. Layer the quilt top, batting, and backing, and pin baste to make a quilt sandwich. Machine or hand quilt as desired. Bind your quilt.

making it fit

I never make the same quilt twice. I do use the same pattern over and over, but never in quite the same way. Sometimes I make it baby size, sometimes twin size. Sometimes I choose a fat border, and sometimes no border at all. Every quilt is different! Here, I'm going to take you through the basics of adjusting any quilt pattern to make it whatever size you want.

QUILT SIZES

First of all, here are general measurements for the following common sizes of quilts:

Baby: 36″ × 36″ (varies)

Throw: Pretty much every size between baby and twin

Twin: 68″ × 86″

Queen: 88″ × 92″

King: 92″ × 108″

THE PERFECT SIZE

It isn't difficult to adjust the size of your quilt; you just have to do a little math. We'll use the *Retro* quilt (page 22) as an example. This quilt has finished blocks measuring 12″ × 12″.

Let's say we want to adjust the size from a 60″ × 72″ throw to a king-sized quilt. Since each block is 12″ × 12″ finished, and we want the quilt to be around 92″ × 108″ finished, we just divide the length and the width by 12.

$92 \div 12 = 7.7$

$108 \div 12 = 9$

If we made the quilt 8 blocks by 9 blocks (again, multiplying each of them by 12), we would come up with a 96″ × 108″ quilt.

Since we now need 72 blocks instead of the original 30, we have to adjust the yardage as well. In this case, the quilt is nearly 2½ times bigger than the original. Knowing that it will be a rough estimate, I would multiply the yardage requirements for the quilt top by 2.5.

CALCULATING BACKING

Backing is simple to calculate; it is simply the area of the quilt. Continuing our previous example, we will calculate the quilt back for our 96″ × 108″ quilt. Most cotton quilting fabric is around 42″ wide, so we'll use that number in our calculation.

Add at least 4″ to the length and width of the quilt for the backing before determining how much you need.

Note: If your quilt will be quilted on a longarm machine, check with your longarm quilter before calculating the extra backing. She or he may require a certain amount of extra fabric on all sides of the quilt. If you are quilting and basting it yourself, 2″ all the way around should be sufficient.

If we divide 112″ (108″ + 2″ + 2″) by 42″, we get 2.7. This means that we need 3 widths of 42″-wide fabric 100″ long (96″ + 2″ + 2″), or 300″ of fabric. 300″ divided by 36″ (because there are 36″ in a yard) is 8.4, so we need 8½ yards of fabric.

BINDING

To calculate the binding, figure out the perimeter of the quilt (length + width × 2). Divide it by 42″. In our 96″ × 108″ quilt example, the perimeter would be 408″.

> 408″ ÷ 42 = 9.7, or (rounding up)
> 10 strips of binding

Note: You may want to add an extra strip just to be safe. (I do! It leaves a little bit for my scrappy binding roll, page 60.)

For yardage, 10 strips of binding 2½″ wide would be 25″ of fabric. 25″ divided by 36″ is 0.7, so we need ¾ yard of fabric.

Adjusting the size of a quilt really isn't a difficult thing to do. It just requires a little practice, a calculator, and maybe some chocolate. Definitely some chocolate!

Dapper

I have three little boys at my house. Two of them are old enough to know exactly what they like. Let's just say that when the mailman dropped off a box of fabric covered in rockets, bicycles, paper hats, and planes, there was an argument or two about who was going to claim the resulting quilt as his own. Of course I had to buy a little more fabric and make two quilts. One is bright, cheery, and colorful (*Dapper Canon*, page 45), and the other (*Dapper Aiden*, page 50) is calm, bold, and sharp. Just like the sweet boys who snuggle under them.

Pieced and quilted by Camille Roskelley

Dapper Canon

FINISHED QUILT: 40″ × 45″ | FINISHED BLOCK: 10″ × 10″

FABRIC: **Children at Play by Sarah Jane Studios for Michael Miller**

Materials

Yardages are based on 42˝-wide fabric.

- 6 fat quarters of coordinating print fabrics for the blocks

- 1½ yards of white fabric for the blocks and sashing

- 1½ yards* of fabric for the backing

- ½ yard of fabric for the binding

- 44˝ × 49˝ piece of batting

* Requires 44˝-wide fabric.

Cutting

From *each* fat quarter:*

Cut 8 pieces 3˝ × 5½˝ (A) and 16 squares 3˝ × 3˝ (B).

From white fabric:

Cut 17 strips 3˝ × WOF.**

- From 7 strips, subcut pieces 3˝ × 5½˝ (7 per strip, for a total of 48) for the blocks (C).

- From 4 strips, subcut squares 3˝ × 3˝ (14 per strip, for a total of 48) for the blocks (D).

- The remaining 6 strips 3˝ × WOF are for the sashing.

From binding fabric:

Cut 5 strips 2½˝ × WOF.

* Each fat quarter yields enough pieces for 2 blocks. Refer to the cutting diagram for help.

** WOF = width of fabric

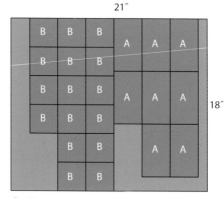

Cutting

BLOCK ASSEMBLY

For each block, you will need 4 matching A print pieces, 8 matching B print pieces, 4 white C pieces, and 4 white D pieces. The block is made up of 4 Flying Geese units and 4 corner units.

1. Refer to Easy Flying Geese (page 49) to make a Flying Geese unit. Make 4 units.

2. Make a corner unit with 1 print A piece and 1 white D piece. Using a pencil, draw a diagonal line from one corner to the opposite corner on the wrong side of each white square. Place a square in a corner of the A piece (a). Sew along the line, and trim ¼˝ from the line on the outside as shown (b). Open and press (c). Make 4 units.

(a)   *(b)*

(c)

Corner unit assembly

3. Sew together 1 corner unit and 1 Flying Geese unit to make 1 quarter-block unit; press. Make 4 quarter-block units. Sew these units together in 2 rows of 2; press. Sew the rows together to make the block; press.

4. Repeat Steps 1–3 to make a total of 12 blocks.

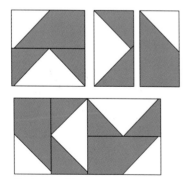

Block assembly

QUILT ASSEMBLY

1. Refer to the quilt assembly diagram to sew the blocks together into 3 columns of 4 blocks each.

2. Measure each column. (If they are different, average them together.) Measure 4 sashing strips the same length. Mark the length with a pin. Sew sashing strips between the columns and on the outsides, as shown in the quilt assembly diagram. Trim excess sashing.

3. Measure the width of the quilt across the top and bottom and through the center. (Again, average the measurements if they are different.) Measure 2 sashing strips the same length. Mark the length with a pin, and sew 1 strip along the top and 1 along the bottom. Trim excess sashing.

Quilt assembly

FINISHING

*Use your favorite methods, or
see Finish It! (page 101).*

1. Make the backing as
described in Backing
(page 103).

2. Layer the quilt top, batting,
and backing, and pin baste
to make a quilt sandwich.
Machine or hand quilt as
desired. Bind your quilt.

easy flying geese

To make a Flying Geese unit, select 1 piece
3″ × 5½″ (C) and 2 squares 3″ × 3″ (B). Using a
pencil, draw a diagonal line from one corner
to the opposite corner on the wrong side of
each B square. Place a square in a corner of
the C piece (a). Sew along the drawn line, and
trim ¼″ from the line on the outside as shown
(b). Open and press (c). Repeat on the opposite
side as shown (d, e, f).

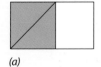

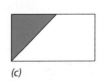
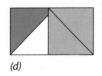
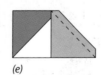
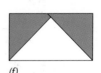

(a) (b) (c) (d) (e) (f)

Dapper Aiden

In this version, the placement of the light and dark fabrics is the reverse of that in *Dapper Canon* (page 45).

Materials

Yardages are based on 42″-wide fabric.

- 1¼ yards of light-colored fabric for the blocks

- 1½ yards of dark-colored fabric for the blocks and sashing

- 1½ yards* of fabric for the backing

- ½ yard of fabric for the binding

- 44″ × 49″ piece of batting

* Requires 44″-wide fabric.

Cutting

From light-colored fabric:

Cut 14 strips 3″ × WOF* for the blocks.

- From 7 strips, subcut pieces 3″ × 5½″ (7 per strip, for a total of 48) (A).

- From 7 strips, subcut squares 3″ × 3″ (14 per strip, for a total of 96) (B).

From dark-colored fabric:

Cut 17 strips 3″ × WOF.

- From 7 strips, subcut pieces 3″ × 5½″ (7 per strip, for a total of 48) for the blocks (C).

- From 4 strips, subcut squares 3″ × 3″ (14 per strip, for a total of 48) for the blocks (D).

- The remaining 6 strips 3″ × WOF are for the sashing.

* WOF = width of fabric

BLOCK ASSEMBLY

For each block, you will need 4 A pieces, 8 B pieces, 4 C pieces, and 4 D pieces.

1. Refer to Easy Flying Geese (page 49) to make a Flying Geese unit with 1 C piece and 2 B pieces. Make 4 Flying Geese.

2. Make a corner unit with 1 A piece and 1 D piece. Using a pencil, draw a diagonal line from one corner to the opposite corner on the wrong side of each D square. Place a square in a corner of the A piece (a). Sew along the drawn line, and trim ¼″ from the line on the outside as shown (b). Open and press (c). Make 4. (Refer to Step 2 illustrations a–c, page 48.)

3. Sew together 1 corner unit and 1 Flying Geese unit to make 1 quarter-block unit; press. Make 4 quarter-block units. Sew these units together in 2 rows of 2; press. Sew the rows together to make the block; press.

4. Repeat Steps 1–3 to make a total of 12 blocks.

ASSEMBLY AND FINISHING

To assemble and finish this quilt, follow the steps for *Dapper Canon* (pages 48 and 49).

...Playground...

We've spent a lot of time at the playground over the last eight years. When my oldest boys were young, we were there just about every day. They loved it there, and I loved how much they loved it! Looking at this quilt in their bedroom reminds me of that playground, where we spent our days when my big boys were little guys—and, well, that I just don't want to forget.

Pieced by Camille Roskelley and quilted by Tami Bradley

FINISHED QUILT: 60″ × 72″ | FINISHED BLOCK: 12″ × 12″

FABRIC: Reunion by Sweetwater for Moda

Materials

Yardages are based on 42″-wide fabric.

- 36 Layer Cake squares 10″ × 10″ for the blocks

- 2¼ yards of neutral fabric for the blocks

- 3⅞ yards of fabric for the backing

- ⅝ yard of fabric for the binding

- 64″ × 76″ piece of cotton batting

Cutting

From Layer Cake squares:

Cut 12 squares into smaller squares 4⅞″ × 4⅞″ (4 smaller squares from each Layer Cake square, for a total of 48) for the half-square triangles (HSTs).*

Cut 24 squares into 4 smaller squares 4½″ × 4½″ (4 smaller squares from each Layer Cake square, for a total of 96) for the blocks.

From neutral fabric:

Cut 6 strips 4⅞″ × WOF;** subcut squares 4⅞″ × 4⅞″ (8 per strip, for a total of 48) for the HSTs.

Cut 10 strips 4½″ × WOF.

- From 7 strips, subcut pieces 4½″ × 12½″ (3 per strip, for a total of 21) for the sashing.

- From 3 strips, subcut squares 4½″ × 4½″ (9 per strip, for a total of 21) for the blocks.

From binding fabric:

Cut 7 strips 2½″ × WOF.

* Each Layer Cake square paired with a neutral square will yield 8 HSTs.
** WOF = width of fabric

BLOCK ASSEMBLY

This quilt is made up of 21 full blocks and 6 partial blocks. First make 96 HSTs using the 48 squares 4⅞″ × 4⅞″ cut from the Layer Cakes and the white squares 4⅞″ × 4⅞″. Refer to Easy HSTs (page 26) for directions.

Half-square triangle

Full blocks

For each of the full blocks, you will need 4 matching HSTs, 4 matching Layer Cake squares 4½″ × 4½″, and 1 white square 4½″ × 4½″.

1. Refer to the full-block assembly diagram to sew together the pieces into 3 rows of 3. Press. Sew together the rows to make 1 full block. Press.

2. Repeat to make a total of 21 blocks.

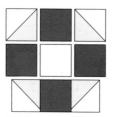

Full-block assembly

Partial blocks

For each of the partial blocks, you will need 2 matching HSTs and 1 Layer Cake square 4½″ × 4½″. Sew together the pieces as shown in the partial-block assembly diagram. Press. Repeat to make a total of 6 partial blocks.

Partial-block assembly

QUILT ASSEMBLY

1. Sew 3 rows A, alternating 4 full blocks and 3 neutral strips 4½″ × 12½″. Press.

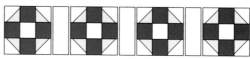

Row A assembly

2. Sew 3 rows B, alternating 3 full blocks and 4 neutral strips 4½″ × 12½″. Sew 1 partial block on each end. Press.

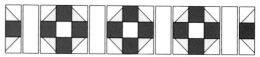

Row B assembly

3. Sew together the 6 rows as shown in the quilt assembly diagram. Press.

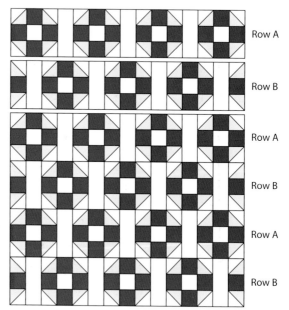

Quilt assembly

FINISHING

Use your favorite methods, or see Finish It! (page 101).

1. Cut the backing fabric into 2 equal lengths (roughly 64″), and sew them together as described in Backing (page 103).

2. Layer the quilt top, batting, and backing, and pin baste to make a quilt sandwich. Machine or hand quilt as desired. Bind your quilt.

Dwell

I've always had a thing for houses. In fact, I graduated from college with a degree in architectural design, and I worked in residential design for several years. I love design, and I love houses. Naturally, house quilts are some of my favorites, because nothing says warm and cozy like home.

Pieced by Camille Roskelley and quilted by Angela Walters

FINISHED QUILT: 51″ × 66″ | FINISHED BLOCK: 9″ × 12″

FABRIC: Scraps from my stash

Materials

Yardages are based on 42″-wide fabric.

- 16 fat quarters of coordinating fabrics or a variety of scraps

- 2⅜ yards* of white fabric for the blocks, sashing, and border

- 3¼ yards of fabric for the backing

- ⅝ yard of fabric or scraps of a variety of fabrics for the binding

- 55″ × 70″ piece of cotton batting

* Requires 42½″ usable fabric width.

Cutting

From white fabric:

Cut 4 strips 5″ × WOF.*

- From 2 strips, subcut squares 5″ × 5″ (8 per strip, for a total of 16) for the blocks.

- From 2 strips, subcut pieces 1½″ × 5″ (28 per strip, for a total of 32) for the blocks.

Cut 4 strips 2½″ × WOF; subcut pieces 2½″ × 12½″ (3 per strip, for a total of 12) for the vertical sashing.

Cut 3 strips 3½″ × 42½″ for the horizontal sashing.

Cut 6 strips 5″ × WOF for the border.

From binding fabric:

Cut 7 strips 2½″ × WOF (or refer to Scrappy Binding (at right).

* WOF = width of fabric

scrappy binding

Every time I finish a binding, I keep the extra pieces and add them to my scrappy binding roll. When I finish a quilt that is just begging for a scrappy binding (like this one), I simply sew the pieces together until I have the correct length. Then I sew it to the quilt.

BLOCK ASSEMBLY

Each block is a basic house motif, but the blocks are not all alike. There are 4 different houses—A, B, C, and D—for you to mix and match. Have fun choosing a variety of fabrics for all the house elements!

House A

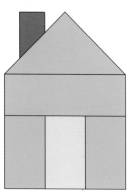

There are 7 of these blocks. For each block, select 3 different fabrics. Note that the roof and chimney for all the houses are constructed later (Roof Construction, page 66).

1. From fabric 1 (main fabric), cut 1 piece 5″ × 9½″ for the roof, 1 piece 3″ × 9½″ for the header, and 2 pieces 3½″ × 5½″ for the walls.

2. From fabric 2, cut 1 piece 3″ × 5″ for the chimney.

3. From fabric 3, cut 1 piece 3½″ × 5½″ for the door.

4. Sew a wall piece to each side of the door piece (a). Sew the header piece along the top (b). Sew the roof piece to the top of the header (c). Press after each addition.

5. Repeat Steps 1–4 to make 7 House A blocks.

(a)

House A

(b)

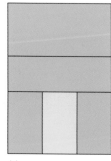

(c)

House B

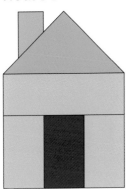

There are 3 of these blocks. For each block, select 4 different fabrics.

1. From fabric 1 (main fabric), cut 1 piece 3″ × 9½″ for the header and 2 pieces 3½″ × 5½″ for the walls.

2. From fabric 2, cut 1 piece 3″ × 5″ for the chimney.

3. From fabric 3, cut 1 piece 3½″ × 5½″ for the door.

4. From fabric 4, cut 1 piece 5″ × 9½″ for the roof.

5. Sew a wall piece to each side of the door piece (a). Sew the header piece along the top (b). Sew the roof piece to the top of the header (c). Press after each addition.

6. Repeat Steps 1–5 to make 3 House B blocks.

(a)

House B

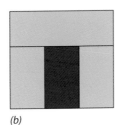

(b)

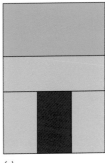

(c)

House C

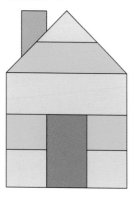

There are 3 of these blocks. For each block, select 4 different fabrics.

1. From fabric 1 (light), cut 1 piece 2½″ × 9½″ for the roof, 1 piece 3½″ × 9½″ for the header, and 2 pieces 3″ × 3½″ for the walls.

2. From fabric 2 (dark), cut 1 piece 3″ × 9½″ for the roof and 2 pieces 3″ × 3½″ for the walls.

3. From fabric 3, cut 1 piece 3″ × 5″ for the chimney.

4. From fabric 4, cut 1 piece 3½″ × 5½″ for the door.

5. Sew 1 dark wall piece to 1 light wall piece along the 3½″ edge to make a wall piece 3½″ × 5½″. Make 2. Sew 1 wall piece to each side of the door (a). Sew the header piece along the top (b). Sew the light roof piece to the dark roof piece, and sew them to the top of the header (c). Press after each addition.

6. Repeat Steps 1–5 to make 3 House C blocks.

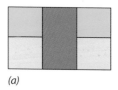

(a)

House C

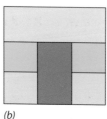

(b)

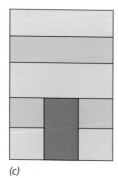

(c)

House D

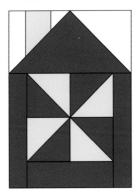

There are 3 of these blocks, which feature pinwheel motifs made using half-square triangles (HSTs). For each block, select 3 different fabrics.

1. From fabric 1 (main fabric), cut 1 piece 5″ × 9½″ for the roof, 2 squares 3⅞″ × 3⅞″ for the pinwheel center, 1 piece 2″ × 6½″ for the floor, and 2 pieces 2″ × 8″ for the walls.

2. From fabric 2, cut 2 squares 3⅞″ × 3⅞″ for the pinwheel center.

3. From fabric 3, cut 1 piece 3″ × 5″ for the chimney.

4. For the pinwheels, make HSTs by placing a fabric 1 square 3⅞″ × 3⅞″ on top of a fabric 2 square 3⅞″ × 3⅞″, right sides together. Follow the directions in Easy HSTs (page 26) to make 4 HSTs. Sew them together in 2 rows of 2. Sew the rows together to make 1 pinwheel. At this point, the pinwheel should measure 6½″ × 6½″.

5. Sew the floor to the bottom of the pinwheel (a). Sew the walls to the sides of the pinwheel (b). Sew the roof to the top of the pinwheel (c). Press after each addition.

6. Repeat Steps 1–5 to make 3 House D blocks.

(a)

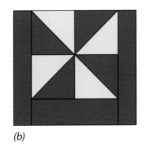

(b)

House D

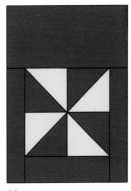

(c)

Roof construction

For all 4 houses, the roofs are finished in the same way.

1. Sew a white piece 1½″ × 5″ to each side of the chimney piece (a). Press. On the back of the square, draw a pencil line from one corner to the opposite corner. Line it up on the roof as shown (b). Sew along the line. Trim ¼″ from the edge. Press to the dark side (c).

2. Repeat Step 1 with a 5″ × 5″ white square to make the other side of the roof (d and e).

3. Repeat Steps 1 and 2 for all 16 house blocks.

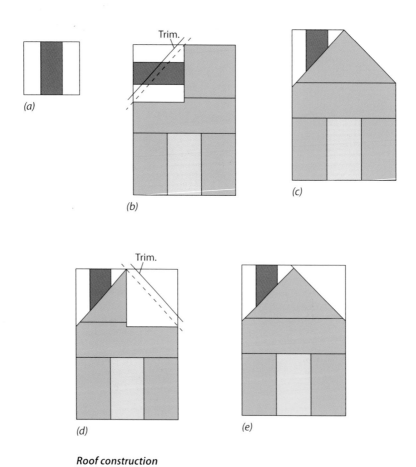

Roof construction

QUILT ASSEMBLY

1. Sew white sashing strips 2½″ × 12½″ between the house blocks as shown in the quilt assembly diagram to make 4 rows of 4. Sew 3½″ sashing strips between the rows as shown.

2. For the border, measure the quilt and follow the process in Tackling Borders (page 101), or use your favorite method for sewing squared borders.

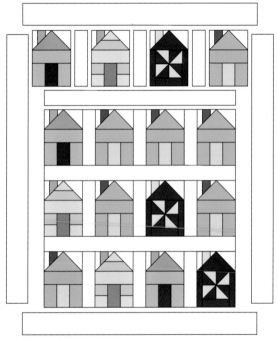

Quilt assembly

FINISHING

Use your favorite methods, or see Finish It! (page 101).

1. Cut the backing fabric into 2 equal lengths (roughly 55″), and sew them together as described in Backing (page 103).

2. Layer the quilt top, batting, and backing, and pin baste to make a quilt sandwich. Machine or hand quilt as desired. Bind your quilt.

Adorn

Sometimes a small wall quilt is the perfect project when life is busy. Just one favorite large block, or a few smaller ones, quilted and bound. This one little star quilt, vintage inspired and hand quilted, holds a special place in my heart. It will always hang in my sewing room, all bright and shiny, a reminder of happy times.

FINISHED QUILT: **22˝ × 24˝**
FABRIC: **Scraps from my stash**

Pieced and quilted by Camille Roskelley

the scrap bin

Overflowing scrap bins—they happen to all of us at one point or another. I'm always on the lookout for a great project to tame mine. This cheery little wall quilt goes together quickly and can use every single one of your very favorite prints. Your scrap bin will thank you.

Materials

Yardages are based on 42˝-wide fabric.

- Scraps or at least 10 different fat eighths for the block

- ⅝ yard of white fabric

- ¾ yard of fabric for the backing

- ⅓ yard of fabric for the binding

- 26˝ × 28˝ piece of cotton batting

Cutting

From scraps or fat eighths:

Cut strips of various widths from 1˝ to 2½˝ for the block.

From white fabric:

Cut 2 strips 5½˝ × WOF* for the block.

Cut 2 strips 3˝ × WOF for the top and bottom border.

From binding fabric:

Cut 3 strips 2½˝ × WOF.

* WOF = width of fabric

BLOCK ASSEMBLY

Template pattern is on page 73.

1. Trace the triangle template pattern onto a piece of paper. Mount it on a piece of heavier paper. Cut it out along the lines to make a template.

2. From your scraps, sew together strips of various widths to make 12 scrappy blocks that each measure at least 6″ × 7″.

3. Using the triangle template, rotary cutter, and mat, cut 12 scrappy triangles.

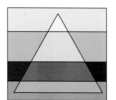

4. From the white fabric strips 5½″ × WOF, cut 12 triangles per strip, for a total of 24, using the triangle template.

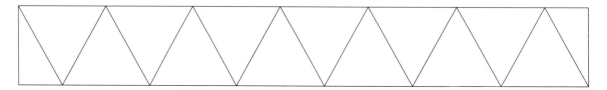

QUILT ASSEMBLY

1. Lay out the triangles as shown in the triangle assembly diagram.

Triangle assembly

2. Sew together the triangles in horizontal rows as shown. Be sure to sew the pieces right sides together, with ¼″ seams. It looks a little tricky, but after you've sewn a few together you'll get the hang of it. Press each seam away from the pieced triangles.

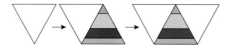

3. Sew together the rows. Press.

4. Once all the rows have been sewn together, refer to the diagram (below) to trim the sides.

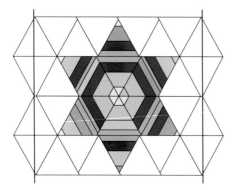

5. For the top and bottom border, measure the quilt and follow the process in Tackling Borders (page 101), or use your favorite method for sewing squared borders.

FINISHING

Use your favorite methods, or see Finish It! (page 101).

1. Make the backing as described in Backing (page 103).

2. Layer the quilt top, batting, and backing, and pin baste to make a quilt sandwich. Machine or hand quilt as desired. Bind your quilt.

Adorn
Triangle
template pattern

Sweet Life

Is there anything better than climbing between fresh, cool sheets after a long day and snuggling under a lovely handmade quilt? Nope, there isn't. Nice, big blocks make it easy to create this generously sized quilt for lots of great snuggling.

Pieced by Camille Roskelley and quilted by Diana Johnson

FINISHED QUILT: 92″ × 92″ | FINISHED BLOCK: 18″ × 18″

FABRIC: Secret Garden by Sandi Henderson for Michael Miller

Materials

Yardages are based on 42˝-wide fabric.

- 16 fat quarters of coordinating prints for the blocks and cornerstones

- 2⅞ yards of white fabric for the blocks and cornerstones

- 2⅞ yards of fabric for the sashing and border

- 8⅜ yards of fabric for the backing

- ⅞ yard of fabric for the binding

- 96˝ × 96˝ piece of cotton batting

mix it up

Since the fabric I picked for this quilt had lots of large-scale prints, I wanted to incorporate some solids. But I didn't want the solids to be the large centers of the blocks. So I used the solids for the small accent triangles and grabbed a few more of my favorite fat quarters for the block centers. It is that simple to adjust your quilt to fit your choice of fabric. Don't be scared to mix things up!

Cutting

From *each* fat quarter:*

Cut 4 pieces 3½˝ × 6½˝ for the blocks.

Cut 4 squares 3½˝ × 3½˝ for the blocks.

Cut 1 square 12½˝ × 12½˝ for the blocks.

Cut 5 squares 1½˝ × 1½˝ for the cornerstones.

From white fabric:

Cut 27 strips 3½˝ × WOF.**

- From 11 strips, subcut pieces 3½˝ × 6½˝ (6 per strip, for a total of 64) for the blocks.***

- From 16 strips, subcut squares 3½˝ × 3½˝ (12 per strip, for a total of 192) for the blocks.

From sashing fabric:

Cut 12 strips 3½˝ × WOF; subcut into pieces 3½˝ × 18½˝ (2 per strip, for a total of 24) for the sashing.

Cut 9 strips 6˝ × WOF for the border.

From binding fabric:

Cut 10 strips 2½˝ × WOF.

* Refer to the cutting diagram (below). Cut carefully!
** WOF = width of fabric
*** Save your scraps for the cornerstones.

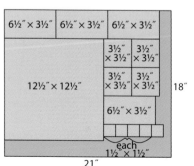

Cutting diagram

BLOCK ASSEMBLY

For each block, you will need 2 different prints. No 2 blocks repeat the same pairs of prints!

1. From fabric 1, choose 1 square 12½″ × 12½″ for the block center. From fabric 2, choose 1 set of 4 pieces 3½″ × 6½″ and 1 set of 4 squares 3½″ × 3½″. Also select 12 white squares 3½″ × 3½″ and 4 white pieces 3½″ × 6½″.

2. Draw a pencil line from one corner to the opposite corner on the wrong side of each of the 4 matching 3½″ × 3½″ fabric 2 squares.

3. Sew a fabric 2 square at each corner of the 12½″ × 12½″ fabric 1 square, along the pencil line, as shown in the block center assembly diagram. Trim the fabric ¼″ from the pencil line. Open and press.

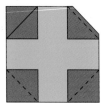 

Block center assembly

4. Using 1 piece 3½″ × 6½″ (fabric 2) and 2 white squares 3½″ × 3½″, make 1 Flying Geese unit. For directions, see Easy Flying Geese (page 49). Make 4 Flying Geese.

5. Refer to the block assembly diagrams to sew a white square 3½″ × 3½″ to each 3½″ side of 2 Flying Geese (a). Sew these to the block top and bottom (b). Sew a white piece 3½″ × 6½″ to each 3½″ side of the 2 remaining Flying Geese (c). Sew these to the sides of the block (d). Press after each addition.

6. Repeat Steps 1–5 to make 16 blocks.

a bonus

Sew together the triangles you trimmed from the Flying Geese to make half-square triangles. Sew these in rows to make a throw pillow top or a small quilt. Yay—free project!

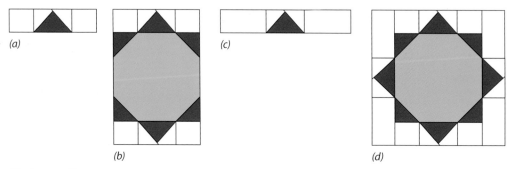

(a) (c)

(b) (d)

Block assembly

QUILT ASSEMBLY

1. For the nine-patch cornerstones, use the scraps of white fabric. From the white scraps, cut 36 squares 1½˝ × 1½˝. Using the fat quarter print squares 1½˝ × 1½˝, make 9 little nine-patches.

Nine-patch assembly

2. Lay out the quilt as shown in the quilt assembly diagram, using the blocks, sashing pieces, and nine-patch cornerstones. Sew the blocks and vertical sashing strips in rows. Sew the sashing and cornerstones in rows. Then sew the rows together, alternating block/sashing rows with sashing/cornerstone rows as shown.

3. For the border, measure the quilt and follow the process in Tackling Borders (page 101), or use your favorite method for sewing squared borders.

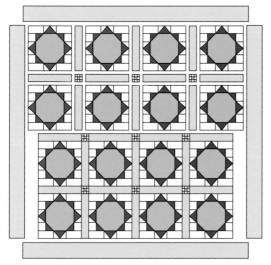

Quilt assembly

FINISHING

Use your favorite methods, or see Finish It! (page 101).

1. Cut the backing fabric into 3 equal lengths (roughly 96˝), and sew them together as described in Backing (page 103).

2. Layer the quilt top, batting, and backing, and pin baste to make a quilt sandwich. Machine or hand quilt as desired. Bind your quilt.

Framed

I'm always on the lookout for quilt designs that can really let large, bold prints shine. They are difficult to find! This design was so fun to draw up, and even more fun to make.

Pieced by Camille Roskelley and quilted by Tami Bradley

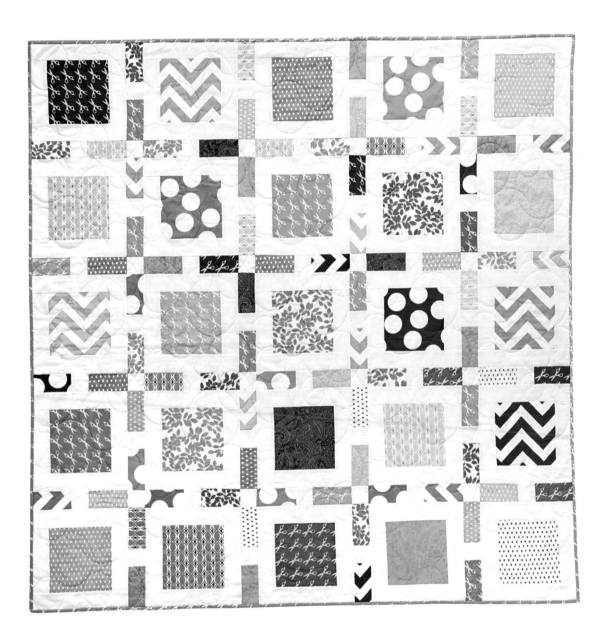

FINISHED QUILT: 63″ × 63″ | FINISHED BLOCK: 11″ × 11″

FABRIC: **Half Moon Modern by Momo for Moda**

Materials

Yardages are based on 42˝-wide fabric.

- 26 Layer Cake squares 10˝ × 10˝ for the blocks and sashing

- 2¼ yards of white fabric for the blocks and sashing

- ⅝ yard of fabric for the binding

- 4 yards of fabric for the backing

- 67˝ × 67˝ piece of cotton batting

Cutting

From 26 Layer Cake squares:

Cut 5 strips 2½˝ × 5˝ from 1 square for the sashing.

Cut each remaining square as shown in the cutting diagram, for a total of 75 strips 2½˝ × 5˝ for the sashing and 25 squares 7½˝ × 7½˝ for the blocks.

From white fabric:

Cut 31 strips 2½˝ × WOF.*

- From 10 strips, subcut pieces 2½˝ × 7½˝ (5 per strip, for a total of 50) for the blocks.

- From 17 strips, subcut pieces 2½˝ × 11½˝ (3 per strip, for a total of 50) for the blocks.

- From 4 strips, subcut squares 2½˝ × 2½˝ (16 per strip, for a total of 56) for the sashing.

quick cuts

When you are cutting a stack of Layer Cake squares, your cutting time will fly if you cut several at a time. Just stack them up and cut through three or four squares at once. Of course, it is a good idea to practice on a few first. Just in case.

From binding fabric:

Cut 7 strips 2½˝ × WOF.

* WOF = width of fabric

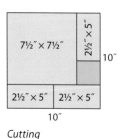

Cutting

BLOCK ASSEMBLY

Refer to the block assembly diagram to sew white strips 2½″ × 7½″ to the top and bottom of 1 Layer Cake square 7½″ × 7½″. Press. Sew a white strip 2½″ × 11½″ to each side. Press. Repeat to make 25 blocks. The blocks should measure 11½″ × 11½″.

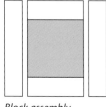

Block assembly

QUILT ASSEMBLY

1. Sew Layer Cake strips 2½″ × 5″ to 2 sides of a white square 2½″ × 2½″ to make a sashing unit. Press. Make 20.

Sashing unit

2. Choose 5 blocks and 4 sashing units. Sew together in 1 row, alternating the blocks and sashing units. Press. Make 5 rows.

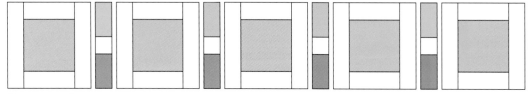

Row construction

3. Choose 10 Layer Cake strips 2½″ × 5″ and 9 white squares 2½″ × 2½″. Sew them into a sashing row, alternating the strips and squares. Press. Make 4 rows.

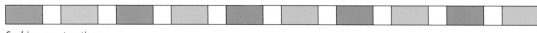

Sashing construction

4. Refer to the quilt assembly diagram to sew the rows together, alternating rows of blocks and rows of sashing. Press.

Quilt assembly

FINISHING

Use your favorite methods, or see Finish It! (page 101).

1. Cut the backing fabric into 2 equal lengths (roughly 67″), and sew them together as described in Backing (page 103).

2. Layer the quilt top, batting, and backing, and pin baste to make a quilt sandwich. Machine or hand quilt as desired. Bind your quilt.

Fresh

This block is one of my absolute favorite quilt blocks. There is something so classic about it, but it's so fresh in a bright, cheery color palette— a perfect example of how you can take some- thing that has been around for almost as long as quilting has and make it new again.

Pieced by Sherri McConnell and quilted by Andrea Marquez

FINISHED QUILT: 96″ × 96″ | FINISHED BLOCK: 24″ × 24″

FABRIC: Marmalade by Bonnie and Camille for Moda

Materials

Yardages are based on 42″-wide fabric.

- 2 Layer Cakes, or 64 Layer Cake squares 10″ × 10″, for the blocks

- 5½ yards of white fabric for the blocks

- 8¾ yards of fabric for the backing

- ⅞ yard of fabric for the binding

- 100″ × 100″ piece of cotton batting

Cutting

From *each* Layer Cake square:

Cut 4 squares 5″ × 5″ for the blocks.

From white fabric:

Cut 15 strips 4½″ × WOF;* subcut squares 4½″ × 4½″ (9 per strip, for a total of 128) for the blocks.

Cut 24 strips 5″ × WOF; subcut squares 5″ × 5″ (8 per strip, for a total of 192) for the blocks.

From binding fabric:

Cut 10 strips 2½″ × WOF.

* WOF = width of fabric

BLOCK ASSEMBLY

Each block is made up of 4 identical units. Each unit is made up of 7 half-square triangles (HSTs) and 2 white squares and has 4 fabrics (a, b, c, and d) plus white fabric.

1. Refer to Easy HSTs (page 26) to make HSTs using a print square 5″ × 5″ and a white square 5″ × 5″. Make 2 fabric a / white HSTs and 2 fabric b / white HSTs. Press. Trim each to 4½″ × 4½″.

2. To make the 3 remaining HSTs, cut the fabric c squares, fabric d squares, and 1 white 5″ × 5″ square in half from one corner to the opposite corner. Sew the triangles together to make 1 fabric c / white HST, 1 fabric d / white HST, and 1 fabric c / fabric d HST. Press. Trim each to 4½″ × 4½″.

Make 2 fabric a / white.

Make 2 fabric b / white.

Make 1 fabric c / white.

Make 1 fabric d / white.

Make 1 fabric c / fabric d.

3. Sew 3 rows of 3 as shown in the unit assembly diagram, using the HSTs and 2 white squares 4½″ × 4½″. Sew the rows together to make 1 unit. Press.

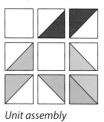

Unit assembly

4. Repeat Steps 1–3 to make 4 units.

5. Sew together the 4 units in 2 rows of 2. Then sew the rows together to make 1 block as shown in the block assembly diagram. Press.

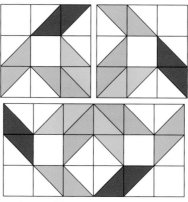

Block assembly

6. Repeat Steps 1–5 to make 16 blocks.

QUILT ASSEMBLY

Sew the blocks in 4 rows of 4. Sew the rows together to make the quilt top, referring to the quilt assembly diagram.

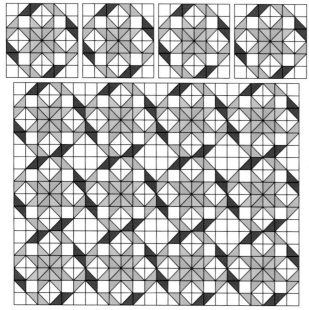

Quilt assembly

FINISHING

Use your favorite methods, or see Finish It! (page 101).

1. Cut the backing fabric into 3 equal lengths (roughly 100″), and sew them together as described in Backing (page 103).

2. Layer the quilt top, batting, and backing, and pin baste to make a quilt sandwich. Machine or hand quilt as desired. Bind your quilt.

wrap-up ··········

At our house, we use our quilts. I mean, we snuggle up on the couch in them, drag them to sporting events, wash them until the binding is about to fall off, and love them to pieces. That's just the way it is over here. Whenever I gift a quilt, I always tell the recipient one thing: Please use it!

CARING FOR YOUR (WELL-LOVED) QUILTS

When your quilts need freshening up, toss them in the washing machine. Just use the gentle cycle and your favorite mild detergent, and you should be good to go. I always wash a few quilts at a time, with a Shout Color Catcher just in case. I also dry them in the dryer on gentle. There are a lot of different views on quilt care, so, for the record, this is only my way of doing things. It has worked well for me over the years. Find what works best for you.

GIFTING IDEAS

It is always a treat to give a quilt to a special friend or family member. I love to roll up my quilts (with the pretty side out) and tie them with a strip of fabric or piece of rickrack. It is a great idea to jot down a few instructions for washing and drying on a note and include it with the card. Tuck the card into the quilt, and you have a thoughtful, personal gift that is sure to be treasured for a very long time.

Lindsay

Quiltmaking
Basics

If you are new to quiltmaking, this chapter will guide you through the basics while offering a few tricks and tips along the way. It would probably be a good idea to read through it all, so if you have a question later on you can refer back to the section you need. Of course, if you know everything there is to know about quilting already (and I'm sure you do), just jump right in to your first project! I'll be right here waiting if you have any questions.

Let's get started....

TOOLS AND CUTTING

Rotary cutters, mats, and rulers

The rotary cutter just might be the greatest quilting invention of all time—after the sewing machine, of course. This fantastic little tool has a circular cutting blade that rolls to cut the fabric quickly and accurately. Once you get the hang of it, you can cut through several layers of fabric at once. Rotary cutter blades are razor sharp, so it is wise to get in the habit of retracting the blade instantly after each cut. That way you reduce the risk of finding out how sharp it really is!

When you use a rotary cutter, you'll need to use a cutting mat along with it. Cutting mats are made of a thick, self-healing material and are very resilient. You will also need a straight acrylic ruler that is roughly the same length as your mat.

Squaring up fabric

Before you begin cutting your fabric, you will need to square it up to ensure accuracy. To do this, fold the fabric in half lengthwise, lining up the selvage edges. Lay the fabric on your rotary mat with the selvages at the top. Align the selvages and the fold parallel to a horizontal gridline on the mat. The left edge of the fabric is where you will begin cutting, with the bulk of the fabric to the right.

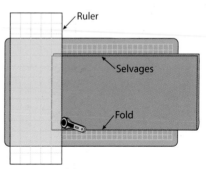

Squaring up fabric

Align a long, straight acrylic ruler with the measurements on the mat. Holding the ruler in place with your left hand, press firmly on the rotary cutter and cut the uneven raw edges along the edge of the ruler. Don't pick up the fabric once it has been squared. Just continue to cut the strips or pieces as instructed in the project instructions.

Cutting strips and squares

CUTTING STRIPS

To cut multiple strips, cut the desired width, starting with the squared edge. Open the cut strips every few strips to make sure they are straight and not crooked. There may be a bump in the middle; if this is the case, stop cutting and square up the fabric again. This will help you to cut straight lines every time.

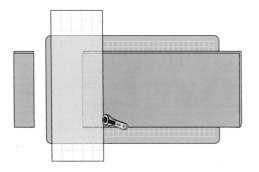

CUTTING SQUARES

When you are cutting squares, you will first cut a strip the appropriate width. Align the strip with the horizontal markings on your cutting mat, and then trim the selvage and square up one end. Continue cutting vertically to get the correct size of square or rectangle.

a little note

WOF means width of fabric. This is measured from selvage to selvage and is anywhere between 42″ and 45″.

PIECING BASICS

As any quilter will tell you, the key to exact piecing is accurate cutting, pinning, and pressing, and a perfect ¼″ seam. And remember, practice makes perfect! We've already covered accurate cutting—now on to pinning, pressing, and perfect seams.

Sewing machine

When choosing a sewing machine for quilting, look for a machine with a nice straight stitch, and possibly a blanket stitch for appliqué. I use a Bernina, and it puts up with me pretty well. Bernina has a wide range of sewing machines, from beginner to professional, and I would definitely recommend any of them.

If your machine is struggling, the problem can usually be solved by simply rethreading the machine and changing the needle. Sewing machines also run better when serviced regularly and kept clean.

Pinning

My pinning technique is pretty simple. As a rule of thumb, I pin every seam intersection. When sewing smaller pieces together, I pin once at the beginning, once at the end, and once in the middle. If the pins are more than 3″ apart, I add additional pins. For more on pinning borders, see Tacking Borders (page 101).

Sewing the perfect seam

THE ¼˝ SEAM ALLOWANCE

Every time you sew 2 pieces of fabric together, you lose ½˝. For example, 2 squares 3˝ × 3˝ sewn together would measure 5½˝ across. This is because in quilting, you use a ¼˝ seam allowance.

The easiest way to get a perfect ¼˝ seam is to use the quilting presser foot for your sewing machine. When using this foot, with the needle in the center position, the fabric only needs to be lined up with the edge of the foot.

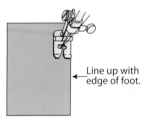

Line up with edge of foot.

To test your ¼″ seam, sew 2 test pieces of fabric together, taking care to line up the straight edge of the fabric with the edge of the quilting presser foot. (If you don't have a quilting presser foot, your sewing machine should have markings on the plate below the presser foot to follow.) With a seam gauge or ruler, measure the seam, and then make any adjustments necessary until the seam measures ¼″.

The best way to get perfect ¼″ seams is to practice. Sew test strips of fabric together until you are confident in your ability to sew straight ¼″ seams.

Pressing

Once you have your perfect ¼″ seam, you will need to press it. Before opening the pieces, you will first press them from the outside to set the stitches. Then open the pieces, and press the seam toward the darker fabric. If the seams need to be pressed a certain direction, this will be specified in the project instructions.

Generally speaking, when 2 seams will be joined, they need to be pressed in opposite directions to create a *locking* or *nesting* seam. Doing this will greatly improve your piecing accuracy.

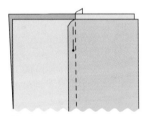

Nesting seams

a little note

Pressing and ironing are two very different things. When you press, lift the iron and place it on the area you'd like to flatten. Don't slide it around; instead, lift it and move it to the next spot. You'll have a lot less distortion and happier piecing all around!

Chain piecing

Chain piecing simply means feeding pairs of pieces, right sides together, through your sewing machine one after another without stopping. Once you have a chain of sewn pieces, snip the threads between the units and press as instructed. This is a huge time-saver, and it can greatly speed up the piecing process.

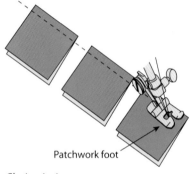

Patchwork foot

Chain piecing

FINISH IT!

Once you get the center of your quilt pieced, it can be tempting to fold it up nicely and put it away for another day. I know I've been tempted to do just that. While putting on borders can be a bit of a pain, it's not nearly as bad as it seems (no pun intended). Follow these steps to finish your quilts, and say good-bye to the closet.

Tackling borders

Borders. Definitely not my favorite part of the quilting process, but certainly a necessity. I've found that if I can get my borders on the right way each time, it makes all the difference in the overall look of the quilt.

To start, cut the number of strips called for in the project instructions to the width specified. If the sides of the quilt are longer than 42˝, you'll need to sew two border strips together for each side.

In order to put the borders on correctly, you will need accurate measurements of your quilt top. In fact, for this reason, I don't give the border measurements in the projects. The first step in preparing the borders is to measure each vertical side of the quilt and measure once down the vertical center. The three measurements should be the same. If they aren't quite the same, take the average of the three lengths and place a pin to mark that measurement on each of the two side borders.

Fold the borders in half lengthwise to find the center (using the pin marking the edge as the edge). Do the same with the quilt top. With the centers and ends aligned, pin the borders

to the quilt top. Add more pins to secure the border to the quilt, distributing the fabric evenly across the quilt top. Sew the borders in place, trim excess fabric, and press. Make sure the corners are square on your cutting mat.

Repeat the process for the remaining top and bottom borders.

See, it's not so bad. And the best part? Perfect borders, every time.

Batting

When choosing a batting, I typically select a 100% cotton batting, such as Warm and Natural (or Warm and White for a white quilt top). I occasionally use an 80/20 blend for a little bit thicker quilt. But as a general rule, I stick with a thin, low- to medium-loft cotton batting.

Backing

The backing is a piece of cake to put together. Just follow the project instructions to cut the correct length, remove the selvages, and join the two pieces to make one piece. Pin and sew a straight line where you trimmed the selvage away, and press the whole thing. For quilts smaller than 42″ in width, you will just use a single piece of fabric cut to the correct length.

The backing and batting need to be at least 2″ bigger on all sides than your quilt top if you are machine quilting or hand quilting it. If you are having it quilted by a longarm quilter, it typically needs to be 4″ bigger all the way around. Ask your quilter before purchasing and preparing your quilt back.

Making a "quilt sandwich"

1. Place the (freshly ironed) backing on a flat surface, wrong side up. Secure it to the surface with masking tape every 8″ or so. Make sure the backing is taut but not stretched.

2. Center and smooth the quilt batting in place on top of the backing.

3. Center the quilt top (also freshly ironed), right side up, on the quilt batting and smooth out any wrinkles, making sure the quilt top edge is parallel with the backing edge.

4. Starting in the center of the quilt, use safety pins to baste the 3 layers together. Pin every 4″ or so, covering the quilt top.

a little note

For hand quilting, use a long needle and thread to baste the layers together, rather than safety pins. Baste horizontally and vertically across the quilt and ¼″ from each edge.

Quilt "as desired"

In this book, I feature quilts with all types of quilting—from hand quilting, to basic machine straight-line quilting and free-motion stippling you can do on your own, to quilting done professionally on a longarm machine.

If you want to learn more about quilting, there are plenty of wonderful books, such as *Machine Quilting with Alex Anderson* (available from C&T Publishing) and *Free-Motion Quilting with Angela Walters* (from Stash Books). Angela is definitely a favorite of mine, and she quilted several of the quilts in this book.

There are so many options for machine quilting and finishing your own quilts, as well as for sending them out. I'll cover just a few favorites here.

Open- and closed-toe darning feet

Walking foot

STIPPLING

This is random, allover free-motion stitching you can do in whatever pattern you choose. Basically, you use a darning foot and lower the feed dogs on your sewing machine so the needle can move around freely. Start in the top right corner and work your way down to the opposite corner, filling in as you go.

a little note

Need a little practice? Practice your stippling skills with pencil on paper. It will help you get used to filling in an area without lifting up your pencil. Go ahead and start doodling. You'll be a pro in no time!

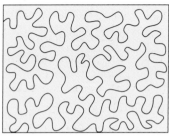

Classic stipple quilting

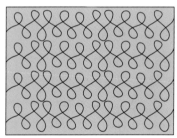

Loops

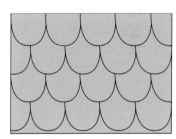

Clamshells

MODERN LINE QUILTING

This is a new favorite of mine. Quilting in rows, either evenly or randomly spaced, adds a modern flair to your design, whether it's modern or traditional. A walking foot that feeds the quilt layers evenly through the machine is a necessity for this kind of quilting. Painter's tape can be a huge help, too. Just place it in straight lines on the quilt top, and follow the tape edge with the edge of the walking foot.

HAND QUILTING

I am far from an expert in hand quilting, but I certainly appreciate the skill behind it and the beauty it gives a quilt. Hand quilting resembles a running stitch that penetrates all three layers. Use a single strand of 100% cotton quilting thread and sew ¼″ away from each seam, or create intricate designs. It's all up to you! Remove the thread basting when you've finished hand quilting your project.

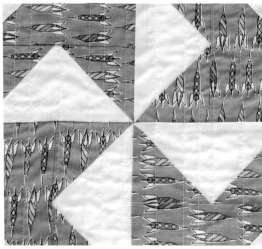

Evenly spaced lines in chevron pattern

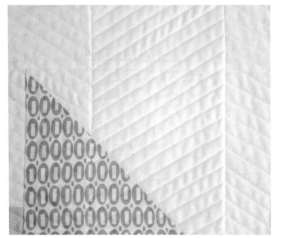

Random straight lines

LONGARM QUILTING

Several of the quilts in this book were quilted by a professional using a longarm quilting machine. With this type of machine, the quilt is stationary, and the quilter moves the machine stitching arm over it. It is especially helpful with larger quilts. If you are having your quilt professionally quilted, there is no need to baste. Check with your quilter for specific instructions.

a little note

After quilting of any type is complete, use a ruler and rotary cutter to trim the backing and batting along the quilt top edges, making sure the corners are square.

Binding

My favorite binding is called a double-fold binding. It is quick and easy, and it gives a nice, crisp edge. For an interesting look, I often bind my quilts in a print or striped fabric. I also love bindings made up of various scraps, as described in Scrappy Binding (page 60).

To bind your quilt, follow these steps.

1. Using a cutting mat, ruler, and rotary cutter, cut the number of strips that the project instructions call for, 2½″ × width of fabric.

2. With right sides together, join the binding strips to make 1 long strip. Press the seams open.

3. Press the strip in half lengthwise, wrong sides together.

4. Stitch the binding to the front of the quilt, aligning the raw edges. Sew through all the layers using a ¼″ seam. Start at the center of one side, leaving a 6″ tail of excess binding.

5. When you approach a corner, stop ¼″ before the corner. Backstitch, and remove the quilt from under the presser foot. Fold the binding upward to create a 45° angle, making sure the edge of the quilt top and binding form a straight line. (a)

6. Hold the first fold in place as you fold and bring the binding back down in line with the next quilt edge. Start stitching at the top of the second fold, and continue stitching on this side of the quilt. Repeat at all the corners. (b)

7. When you come back to where you started, stop stitching 6″ before the end. Fold the ending tail of the binding back on itself where it meets the beginning binding tail. From this fold, measure and mark ½″. Cut the ending binding tail to this measurement. (c)

8. Open both tails. Place one tail on top of the other, with right sides together. Pin. Stitch together with a ¼″ seam allowance. Press open. (d)

9. Refold the binding and finish stitching it to the quilt.

10. Bring the folded edge around to the back of the quilt, miter the corners, and hand stitch in place.

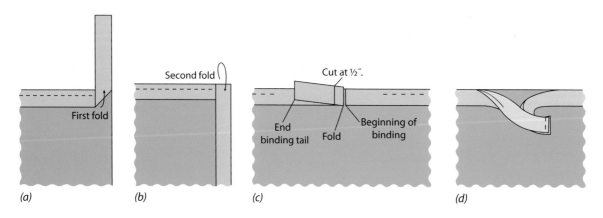

(a)   (b)   (c)   (d)

meet the author

Quilting and design have been a part of my life for as long as I can remember. I grew up in a home that was brimming with quilts and creativity. My mother, Bonnie Olaveson, can attest to the fact that I was constantly working on all sorts of projects (many of them secret, much to her chagrin), some turning out … better than others.

When I began my company, Thimble Blossoms, my main purpose was to have an outlet, a place where I could fulfill my desire to create something original—something that might help inspire others to recognize their creative potential as well.

Since starting my business in 2007, I have designed more than 50 original patterns and have written two books.

My mother (owner of Cotton Way) and I were asked to design fabric for Moda in 2008, and we have designed six fabric lines so far—Cotton Blossoms, Simple Abundance, Bliss, Ruby, Vintage Modern, and Marmalade. Working with Moda has been an amazing experience, and we couldn't be happier about being a part of the Moda crew. I say it every day: best job ever.

I've been blogging since 2006, and I absolutely love the creative community that blogging provides. I blog about quilting, raising a family, and life in general. I have three little boys and one sweet husband. They make my life pretty great *and* really crazy! I love a good treat, sewing nights with friends, taking photos, steak tacos, and weekend getaways to the beach with my family.

Life is sweet. Crazy, but sweet.

Camille

WEBSITE thimbleblossoms.com
BLOG camilleroskelley.com

Retro

reminiscent
of things past